Real Life Poetry
"Something For Even You"

sheryl d. madison

TATE PUBLISHING & *Enterprises*

"Real Life Poetry: Something for Even You" by Sheryl D. Madison

Copyright © 2006 by Sheryl D. Madison. All rights reserved.

Published in the United States of America
by Tate Publishing, LLC
127 East Trade Center Terrace
Mustang, OK 73064
(888) 361-9473

Book design copyright © 2006 by Tate Publishing, LLC. All rights reserved.

The opinions expressed by the author are not necessarily those
of Tate Publishing, LLC.

ISBN: 1-5988647-0-X

060616

ENDORSEMENTS

I have known Sheryl Madison since 1995. She is very kind-hearted, generous, and sprinkled with a wonderful sense of humor. I've also had the opportunity to observe Sheryl grow stronger in her Christian faith. She has overcome and persevered through many tragedies in the past few years. Sheryl has used her remarkable poetic talents in helping others overcome tragedies in their lives. Her poetry is inspirational and soothing to the soul. I thank God for her wonderful friendship. May this book written by Sheryl through the inspiration of our Lord Jesus Christ help and encourage others along their earthly journey. God bless you.

Sister-in-Christ,
Miranda Murrell

Words cannot describe Sheryl. Her presence speaks for itself only in a lifetime do you meet someone that God has put in your path. She is so soft spoken, so matter-of-fact when God has spoken to her. Sheryl is the type of individual that will lead you down the right path. Thank you for everything.

Gwen Berkwitt

The poems in this book are about everyday life, readers will find a poem or two, which will make them stop and ask, "How does Sheryl know this about me?" You'll be personally affected by some poems before you have finished the book.

Juanita Cornette

The poetry that Sheryl writes touches your heart and your spirit. Her poems are a reflection of her emotional and spiritual journey, and how trusting in the Lord can give hope when you feel hopeless.

Athena Powell

The goal of Sheryl Madison's presentation of poems is that they will serve as an inspiration and guidance to every reader who realizes they are words of a woman who has experienced many struggles and trials in life. She has sought to inspire others and to glorify God with her poems.

In this book, there is "something for even you", so I encourage every one to read this book and pass it on.

Sharon Taylor

I have known Sheryl Madison for over 10 years. She is a very loving and giving person, always willing to lend an extra hand whenever needed. I am proud to call her my friend.

Sincerely,
Belinda Bugg

FOREWORD
By Reverend Marticia D. Banks-Booker

All of our daily living is poetic. Poetry is important to our living, and it becomes more important to recognize its effects. Poems can inspire and make us think about God, mankind, the human race. By just spending a few minutes meditating on the thoughts or words in a poem each day, new insight can be revealed, and our possibilities become unlimited. Poetry has become very essential in the lives of Christians because they reflect experiences and touch us at a personal level.

I know this book has its own uniqueness because the selected poems were written by an individual in a category all of her own. Her prose in poetical form and sound were written for others to read, study, listen to, and enjoy.

Listening to poetry can encourage the discouraged or disconsolate soul. Please allow the book of poems to become a vital source of pleasure. It is my prayer and heart's desire that this book of poems becomes an important and enriching part of your ministry and life.

ACKNOWLEDGEMENTS

Real Life Poetry – Something for Even You is a dedication to my God. Abba my father has not only brought me through the many trials and tribulations you'll read about, but He's given me the talent to be able to write about them in the form of poetry. Gifts and talents are given to share with others. I am sharing those that were given to me. Although I will never arrive, because of the trials, tests, and circumstances strategically placed in my life, I am no longer where I used to be. Glory be to God. Each day is a fight to be more like Jesus, my Savior, and my King. Follow Him and just sit back and watch what He can do. Thank You Lord.

Through the years many have entered and exited my life. If only leaving a small impression on my heart, it's significant and I say thank you. I want to say thank you to Janice Reese for encouraging me to write. Who knew it would lead to this. Although God has blessed me with many and I won't be able to name them all, I thank all of my friends that have been there for me and you know who you are. Thanks go out to Belinda Bugg for not only typing my poems when I only had two but also for the quiet friendship love we've shared for more than 15 years. I want to thank Jose Arita who has been like a brother to me. He, as well as his mother Miss Cora, has watched out for me for many years. Jose's not only been like a brother, he's also been a friend. Because of previous military ties I have no family in the vicinity, yet it feels as though I do.

Miranda Murrell has treated me for the past ten years like a sister, a friend and a business partner. Thanks to her husband Richard also. In my God given ventures, she said yes, allowing God to use her as a vessel. Thanks be to God. Thanks is given to my co-workers and management who have had encouraging words and had to listen to me read. Thanks go out to Gwen Berkwitt my beautician and friend from VeeGees as she had on many occasions customers lined up not only to get their hair done, but to hear me read. Thanks for the opportunities. I want to thank Pastor Lee Fields and Grace Fellowship of Columbus, Georgia for all the support given me during the darkest time of my life. Thank you Juanita Cornette for typing and re-typing, never giving up on me. Mrs. S. Taylor, all I can say is thanks so much for everything. The Peralta family, Eileen, (Celeste "Mama," now deceased) and the rest of the clan, thank you for making me one of the family. I love and miss Alex Peralta, deceased March 27, 2004. Many thanks to Reverend Marticia Banks-Booker, my spiritual leader and friend, who prayed me through the worst times of my life. She not only inspired me but so did her mother the late Ms. Bertha Wilborn. Thank you is in order for my church, the Fort Belvoir Gospel Service, where much of my spiritual growth was obtained. Erick Lenard LaShaun Madison, my son. What a special son you are. Kudos goes out to you for being the kind of son that has allowed me to have the time and peace to do this book because I didn't have to worry about you. You are a nice young man. Always follow God and you will always be alright. Acknowledgements go out to my brothers and sister, nieces and nephews, the Overton clan: Billy, Kevin, Mitchell, Tanya, Shekiva, Angel, Terrance Immanuel and Trinity. May God continue to bless and keep you all.

My mother Rose Overton was my biggest fan as I was hers. She was my best friend and I loved her dearly. She kept me well through her prayers and when she passed away I nearly died. Suddenly I found myself in a place that many have visited involuntarily. The place is called rock bottom. Grief sent me, but depression kept me there. All because of the positive affect my mother, the ordained minister had on me that I knew I would no longer be able to receive. Like my heart, my world was torn to pieces. But then God lovingly pulled me out of that mess. Five and a half years later I still want to cry, not because of grief, but because I am so grateful for what the Lord has done for me. No matter your situation or who you are if Jesus is your Lord and Savior – trust and believe and He will turn that thing around. If you have not yet made Him Lord over your life and wish to do so, all you have to do is believe in your heart, confess with your mouth that Jesus died, was raised from the dead, ask for forgiveness of your sins, repent (turn-away) from your sins, ask Jesus to come into your heart and receive Him, seek the Lord diligently, go to a bible based church and read the bible. This is all that is required of you. God will do the rest.

Thank you for purchasing my book.
May the Lord Bless you Abundantly.

In Loving Memory of My Mother

ROSE OVERTON

20 May 1937 - 28 June 2000

I'm just another ordinary person the
devil tried to take out,
but God did what He said He would do.
He turned what the devil meant for harm to good.
Not only did He restore my
spiritual, physical and emotional health, but
He's given me the talent to write my life in poetry
form. All the poems are true and have been
created not just for your entertainment
but to let you, the reader know, you are not alone.
More importantly God will do for you
what He's done for me.
He's a non-respecter of persons.
Glory be to God!

May These Words Give the Hopeless, Hope.

CHAPTER ONE

Although this chapter is short, it is the most special to me. It is a tribute to my mother, whom also was my best friend. She inspired me and I loved her dearly. After her brief illness, she passed away June 28, 2000. I thought I was going to die. Nine months later, because of stress and depression, I actually was told I would die. Thanks to God's grace I am still here.

MOTHER IS THE TITLE
❧

Mother is the Title
given to all
Who's ever, birthed, a child
But mother means much
more to me
And I can tell you how.
Your love, your care,
your soothing words
That eases me when I'm
down
And I would give up anything
to always have
you around
I know the miles are many
that come between us both
But love can see
no distance
When we need each other
most
I hope that what you've
given me
I can give it in return
The love that you have
given me
I hope that I have
earned

I wouldn't trade you
for the world
I hope you'll always know
I thank you God
for giving me
My mother who's called
ROSE

MOTHER KEPT ME

My Mother kept me very well
In all my wicked ways through prayerful pleas
To God our Lord
I would accept one day
She prayed for me, day and night and during my darkest hours
Because I did not follow Him
I had no strength or power
She was the one who did it all because she had such favor
Mom kept me well
From pleas to Him
It wasn't from my labor
God answered my Mother's pleas for me
To keep me going strong
But then He said, "The day will come when you will think I'm wrong,
The fact is child; your Mom's fulfilled all her jobs and duties
 It's time for her to be with Me, Jesus, and Heavens beauty."
Yes, He was right, right from the start
With everything He said
My Mom went home with Him that night and I began to dread
Each day that passed I felt like dying because I was torn to pieces
The only thing I seemed to do well was crying and eating Reese's
I got so fat; I got so down
They told me I was going to die
It still didn't matter much to me until God told me why
He said, "You don't value Life," You're right my God, I said to
Him My transformation began that day

With just a simple grin
I knew I had to stand on my own
Without my Mom around
But since I've stood I'm not alone
The Three in One I've found
So thank you Mom for all your pleas
To God in Heaven above
I'm standing strong and passing it on
All thanks to you and your love

Dedicated to the Memory of

ROSE OVERTON
My Loving Mother

A MOMENT IN TIME

June 28, 2000
Wasn't just another ordinary day
The past 12 hours had been spent
Hoping, praying, and begging God
to see things my way
You see my mom was in a euphoric state
Not really gone, yet not really here
And even though she wasn't,
I was continuously in a state
Gripped with fear
And in spite of the only movement
Was tears running down her face
I still believed she would be okay
Because of God's wonderful grace
But, at approximately eight forty five
All time seemed to have stood still
Not another breath
Was taken by my mom
 No more would I be able to feel
The love my mom had given me
Throughout my 42 years
I shed much more than tears that night
And took on the spirit of fear
The loss of my mom was so very hard
I lost my will to live
For a moment in time

I was out of my mind
I hoped we could reunite again

It's You and Me Sam

It's you and me Sam
Who knew that a borrowed line
From an old Bogart movie
Would linger in the heart
Of a mother's daughter
These were the words
My mom would say to me
Once everyone left
Including my brother
She knew that I would stick by her
No matter what we faced
Things got hard and things got bad
But thanks to God's given grace
We faced each day
One at a time
And made each one of them count
No place else I would rather be
And my mother never had any doubt
I became what she needed
Day by day
So happy she still was around
I loved her so
And she did know
That's how the phrase came about

Role Reversal

As a small child
I remember so clearly
 My mother taking care of me
 She did all I needed
 I've always been treated
With love and respect you see
But then came a time
No more in her prime
Her body began to fail
I took on the role
With body and soul
To help her begin her trail
Back to good health
We really were hoping
That she would regain her form
 It never did happen
But she kept on clapping
I cared for her till she was gone

CHAPTER TWO

I give all glory and honor to my Father God. He's given me an unlimited source of words and has arranged them in a rhyming format. Because all these poems are true stories, through these tragedies, God has done exactly what His word says He will do. Turned to good what the devil meant for harm. Glory to God!

STAND

❧

Lord, let your saints not get weary
during the trials that are to come
The load sometimes feel heavy, too much
For only one
Then weakened by the devil and the
Destruction that he cause
He'll kill you if he gets a chance
Especially if you run for God
The more you lead the people
From this sinful world of his
Test after test will come your way
But you can pass each quiz
The devil is strong and he can cause
All kinds of trouble and confusion
But we have God almighty Lord JESUS
The Holy Spirit who's no illusion
So the next time that you're feeling weak
And ready to bow out
Remember God is on your side
And continue to stay His route
The rewards are many starting with
The salvation gift to you
Although this is the best one
There are many others too
But stand we must, throughout it all
We know the end of the story

And watch how God will work through us
And show His awesome glory

Not By Works

The abundant life is what
God wants
for each and every one of you
But many times we seem to think
we can earn it
through the works we do,
We work real hard and give a lot
to the Kingdom
that belongs to God.
Sometimes overlooking the fact
that we still won't get the nod,
of well done
my good and faithful servant
of which we want to hear,
for lack of knowledge
of God's people
we struggle with things and fear.
You see the real way
to achieve abundant life
on this earth
Establish an intimate and sincere
relationship with God,
It's not by your works.

Inside Hurts

There's obviously no evidence, by
a dressing or a wrap
Not even a small little band-aid, or limbs
held up by a strap
You see no scars or wounds,
that show some sign of pain
There's not even an expression on
her face, that says I hurt again
So look you must past skin and flesh
past organs and the bones
Go straight to the heart look deep within
the place called JESUS' home
You'll find many hurts that's been
living there for quite a long, long time
And although, not very easy to see with time can
mess with your mind
But JESUS loves you so very much
HE wants to set you free
From all that junk, that's been stored up
that the devil wants you to keep
Just let HIM have HIS way with you
You'll see what all HE can do
Rejoice you will because you'll feel
set free and so brand new

STRUGGLES

Struggles I do have many
And I know the reasons for them
I'm close to my blessings from God
Now I'm really leaning on Him
I passed my test last week
After the sixth or seventh time
Thank God for me and others
That Our Father's really kind
The devil's coming at me
From the left and from the right
He used to win all battles
Now I send him on a flight
God said if you resist him
That he'll turn away and flee
I stomp the devil's head
And tell him, don't you mess with me
My courage comes from God above
And Jesus my Lord and Savior
Since my baptism at my church
I notice I have more favor
So now when things get a little hard
And do not go my way
I know I'm one step closer
To my blessings that I prayed

Two Separate Views

My life as is can be looked at
in two separate point of views
It's up to me
which one I believe
and which one will I choose
I rent a room inside a home
that doesn't belong to me
I drive an old Geo Metro
It's a 1993
I have four other siblings
that I really don't know well
Although we grew up together
at home they didn't want to dwell
My mother, who was my best friend
became ill and passed away
My mother's sister, I called Aunt Bay
she died the same old way
I nearly died in between these deaths
because of stress and worry
And when they said that I would die
I really wasn't sorry
And then my love
My one and only
Succumbed to a cancerous disease
By now any normal person would be saying
God stop this madness please

Money in the bank
I don't have much
and soon it will be gone
Just looking at this view
of my life
I wish I wasn't born
But now let's take the other approach
and see what we can see
After accepting Jesus in my life
I'll tell you what God's done for me
I found a room in someone's home
that was very close to my job
I'll keep on driving that 93
until God gets me a brand new car
My relationships with
each of my brothers and sister
is being restored
and all my loved ones
who've passed away
are in Heaven that's for sure
You see where I am
is not where I'll stay
my God has many
plans for me
My enemies and tragedies
are strategically placed
to mold me into
What He wants me to be
I can honestly say
I have joy everyday
Just knowing that God's on my side

Starting today
from now on I pray
Start looking at what's
right in your life

Bearing More Fruit

Bearing more fruit is the
subject of this poem.
Being attached to the vine
is having Jesus as your home
Loving one another is a thing
that we must do
Works are an important part
of discipleship that we do too
Developing Christ-like character
we cannot do, without
cause every move you make
there's someone watching
you no doubt
I left-the service that night
planning to share it with
my friend
I went straight to her shop and
I saw her, a lady and a man
I shared my fruit on both accounts
including the ones you eat
They ate some grapes from the
basket I won cause a sticker
was on my seat
But most of all the words
I shared they said meant
much to them

Ionly repeated what I heard
from a Minister I call friend
After about an hour or so
I decided I should go
But then I mentioned the Minister's
name and the man said
oh I know
the person that you're talking
about has really got it together
Thank God for me my fruit were
good and my words were even
better
I learned an important lesson that
night of which she already said
Stay connected to the vine or
else your fruit will be dead.

Two Obedient Servants

In spite of me
Being the only one in there
and all the many chairs
were empty everywhere
The Minister still taught the class
He did prepare
Because his boss the Chaplain said
He was aware
Of knowledge new believers
Needed to be shared
But God had another plan
For class that night
I had two minister teachers
Showing me the light
For a problem that has been
Freshly in my life
It caused me much confusion
That wasn't
Really right
I left the classroom that night
Feeling really free
After all the bible verses
That she showed me
That's why obedience to God is always the key
Now I know why the class was filled
With only three.

SENT

I know, You sent me to help her
with the visions she has in her heart
From the extreme and unending willingness
and the sincerity of doing my part
How come she can't seem to accept it
that YOU'D love her enough to do this
or is it the fear of being successful
in all of the things that she wished
Perhaps she's been let down by many
In time expecting the same out of me
No matter how many tests that she puts me through
I'll still be around wait and see
I come in the name of my JESUS
No hidden agendas to be found
With time and my loving God's guidance
She'll see that I'm on solid ground
so if I appear to be pushy
and focused with eyes on the prize
The prize is bringing many
Souls to JESUS
stopping the lies of the devil that time is on their side

My Testimony

I used to hear the testimony
of many others
Didn't follow God so I couldn't
really hear
Appearing to really hear the words
of my Minister mother
Apparently not, because I had
no fear
Of living life continuously
with sinful natures
And taking chances with my
destiny
The sinner's life will lead to a
death filled wager
You know where I will spend
eternity
I once was in the governments
U.S. military
and had to follow all those
in command
I'm now a member of
God's Christian army
and now I follow JESUS
the only God-Man.
The testimonies that I hear
now changed a lot

Not because GOD doesn't do the same
It's just that GOD has changed me
like you mold a pot
Now the testimonies that I hear
I claim.

God's Gifts

❧

God's given me gifts
Of great, great magnitude
Only able to receive them
Once I've changed my attitude
I used to get angry daily at others
And then I remembered
The words of my mother
She had such joy, peace, and tranquility
I knew what I needed, to suffer humility
I began to humble myself and to help others
The task wasn't easy, but in order to uncover
The junk that was stored up in me for years,
Eventually came out, but not without tears
God cannot use you without the right heart
He'll change you, remake you
He'll mold you like a pot

Ex- Depressed

The tragedy that made me
What I am today
The very thing that made me
Turn the other way
The thing that turned
my world upside down
that made my unlimited smile
turn to a frown
It caused me headaches
and pain in my heart
Each day became harder
and harder for me
to get up and start
In a crowded room
I still felt all alone
Friends called,
I wouldn't even answer the phone
My eating habits suddenly became
Out of control
I ate everything
As if my stomach had a hole
All these things finally began
To take it's toll

But God knew the way to help me
Was to save my soul
So after they told me
I was going to die this day
My Father God visited me
With four words to say You don't value life
Is what He said to me
just enough words
to start me thinking, you see
My mind began to change
Then my heart started to heal
I took Jesus into my heart
He kept His part of the deal
He turned my life completely around
No more bondage of being down
No matter what it is
That tries to steal your joy
God can turn that bad thing
Good
And keep you from being destroyed
So when you think
Your life is hard
Remember, There's nothing too hard
For God

WHY ME?

Why me, is what I said
When my Mother left this earth
How come God healed many others
Didn't my Mom have worth?
I was angry and I was down
I didn't feel any love
Especially from the God above
Who said that He so loved, the world
He gave his only son
To wash our sins away
But why God why
You didn't heal, my Mom
So she could stay
But then I changed and I could see
What God had done for me
He let my Mom not stay sick long
Before she went to be
With God the father
And God the son
In all of heavens beauty
The only time I say why me
Is why you love me truly

ROCK BOTTOM

I've been to a place
Many have been before, Yet it's not a place
Any of us can say we adore
I went there when my Mother died many have been there since
While I was there I cried and cried
I don't want to take a chance
Of ever returning to this place
That gives you only two choices
 The one - will be to die right there
Or two - to hear the voices
Of God pulling you out of that place With His long and out-
stretched arm
He loves you dearly in spite of yourself
He'll keep you from going this far

YOUR LIFE'S A MESS

Your life's a mess
And all seems wrong
Each day that passes
The nights are long
Your friends are gone
Your family's left
No one can deal with this big test
You need someone to help you through
The once called friend
You thought you knew
It's drugs for me
It's booze for you
It's sex for others, and stealing too
No matter what the thing is called
There is a name above it all
The name is JESUS CHRIST our Lord
Just ask HIM please
To come in your heart
HE'LL be the only friend you'll need
To get you through
And you'll succeed
Cause JESUS is a friend to all
To whom all answers
When HE calls

INDEPENDENT PERSON
❧

I've always been an independent person
Full of pride and attitude
But during the times when things went wrong
And my life was full of gloom
I had no money, and my health was bad
My zest for life was gone
I worked too hard
I had no time
For anyone I loved
But still I did not call out
To Jesus Christ, Our Lord
I thought I could do it on my own
Like many times before
Deeper and deeper and weaker I got
As depression set all about me
Until one day I could stand no more
A sense of inadequacy
I cried out loud to God above
Please help me if you can
He said to me: I love you child
Just confess to who I am
I did exactly what He said
And praised Him day and night
He said: I sent for you,
My Son
So everything can be all right

I knew right then that I was free
Through the precious blood of Jesus
I'll try until the day I die
To become one of His pleasers
So when you're feeling down and out
And not right for the part
Remember one thing forever more
You too are special to God

THE TEST - THE SEED

I have so many problems and they're
Mounting all up on me
I found out just this past week
I owe the IRS some money
My job has just informed me that
they want to give me more duties
as an EEO representative more money
is not included
But worst of all I got a call which
could be bad and good
They want me to take custody of my niece
and I really felt that I should
the problem is I don't have the money
or a place for her to live
The state of Virginia won't help me much
in spite of the taxes I give
So the answer to all when you begin to fall
from the weight of all your problems is to sow a seed, but you
must believe
That our Father God really will solve them

Proverbs 3:5-6
*Trust in the Lord with all your
Heart; lean not on your own understanding.
In all your ways acknowledge Him and
He will direct your paths.*

I LOVE JESUS

I love you Jesus
Right from the heart
This wasn't the story
At the start
Oh yes I knew
About Him and His love
And of His name
No name above
How He sacrificed
His body for me
So that today
I could be free
How He called me
To be one of His own
Then showed me the love
That wasn't at home
He kept me through the years
And years of turmoil
Bad health, no wealth
Jehovah Jireh

OH MIGHTY GOD

Oh mighty God of all
You created us in your
Image
But then because of
 Our fall
Our relationship became
Limited
You wanted fellowship
Between us both
But we're the ones
Who broke the oath
Instead of wiping out
The human race
You showed your love
And gave us grace
You made yourself into
Your Son
You came from heaven
Became the one
You sacrificed your life
For me
And now today I'm truly
Free
In case a person wants
To know
You are the only way

To go
Accept him in your heart today
No longer, fear is in your
Way
He'll give you hope, love
grace, and peace
You'll find that you're
 No longer weak.

I CAN REMEMBER

I can, remember, the days,
That I was made,
To go, to church
I also remember when
My job was first
So on Sundays I
Went to work
I knew of His name
And all that he claimed
But thought I wasn't
Ready to convert
From sinner to saint
Worldly things seemed great
But not after suffering that
Pain
The loss of a loved one
Can cause you to run
To the left or right
Extreme
Choose life, not death
God's there, you bet
He'll help you continue your dreams

LATE? TOO LATE

I thought I had another day
Lots of pleasures come my way
I would be asked and I would say
Let's do it again today
It felt so good; it was great fun
Not knowing all the harm I'd done
Living life as though I thought
That I was Number One
This path can only last so long
But then you'll see what's all gone wrong
When bodily you are stricken right away
No more time to change your mind
Which then means you'd be left behind
Because now it's become
Your judgment day

What If

What if
God never sent
His Son
To be that bridge to eternity
We all were responsible for
our own sins
When we reached that Judgement
Day
Would the world still be
existing today
The way we know it now
Or would the world be
full of ashes
mashed in the ground?
Thank God he did not
go this route
And now we have a
choice
To cross that bridge
to eternity
And hear His sweetest
Voice

THE LIGHT

The stench of my own foolish pride
Feeling I'm so good I need not be saved
Living a life that leads to nowhere
Enjoying my secular parade
Living in darkness and fear
While allowing loneliness to move in
I don't really want to be here
But it's not yet time for my end
My past doesn't have to determine my future
I don't have to stay in the dark
Just turn on the switch
To the Light of the World
Ask Him for a brand new start

JEALOUSY
❧

You see someone that has
an anointing, and full
of fire for the Lord
Instead of saying, she thinks
she's something and using
your tongue like a sword
You lift her up and give
her love just as God says
we should do
You'll find that you have
gifts and talents
That God didn't skip over you
Jealousy is not a spirit
of God there's really
no need for it
Reverse that spirit, turn it
to support you'll see
how much you've sown it
when you become her because
your anointing has
fallen heavily upon you
Now it's your turn to go through
The burn another jealous person
Wants to be you

Trust In Him

Suddenly my heart became heavy
Overwhelmed with a deep grieving pain
not because I don't have any money
or funds to fix my car once again
Not even because my invention
Has yet to receive a contract
although my sweet fourteen year
old niece Angel is in a group home
No it's not that
My job is too strenuous and dirty
and the pay is not close
to what I need
For some this could be very painful
but even this isn't causing me to grieve
I'll tell you exactly what I realized
After finishing class the last night
Trusting in the Lord with all your heart
I found out I wasn't doing it right
So I'm sorry dear Father please forgive me
For not really counting only on you
but now that I know what I need to do
This list belongs to You cause I'm through

MEGA CHURCH

Preaching over a mega church
Is what many want to do
But don't you know
The anointing is there in a small church too
Being well known
Television shows
Flying from place to place
God can use
The vessel He choose
Without you ever leaving that state
Money to buy whatever you want
and services you'd like to have
But can that same money
Buy your salvation
and if it could
Would you be glad
As many musicians and choirs around
And programs of step and dance
Would you be satisfied if
you had none of these
Just an anointed man
The object of this story is to tell you, my friend
It's not where you are today
All of these are right
God set the sights
What matters is how many souls
Can you sway

Wanna Be Like Jesus

JESUS make me more like YOU
every day
these are words you've heard
many people say
Then someone comes to them for
a helping hand
They'll only do it if it doesn't
mess up their plan
But I tell YOU LORD I mean it
with all my heart
I'm not waiting for financial
blessings just to start
Help me to help the ones YOU
send my way
cause helping others really
makes my day.

Thanks Lord

GOD

✿

Who commanded the rain to start
And stop after dispersing 1.5 inches
Of water
GOD
Who decided that you would get
Up feeling alive just like you
Thought you oughta
GOD
Who created a host of trees with
Different types of leaves that sway
In the wind but never falling over
GOD
Who said to the darkness
Let there be light and there was
GOD
Who taught the wasp and the bees that they
Don't whistle but that they buzz
GOD
Who showed me that anger,
Vengefulness and unforgiveness
was wrong then showed me
What love does
GOD
Who made this earth far enough
Away yet close enough to other
Planets and not get crushed

GOD
Who made this earth so perfect
In every way that when you go around it
you don't fall off
GOD
Who wanted a companion and
Decided to make one of His very own
With dust and a puff
GOD
Who gave to you His life on
A cross, suffering for all,
Don't think it wasn't tough
GOD

HAPPY
❧

Happy is the heart
That has been mended by God
After a tragedy has occurred
Happy is the soul that now
Belongs to the Lord
After a lifetime of living absurd
Happy is the joy you feel
Because God has given you peace
Even while your life is full of strife
Happy is the grace and mercy
He dishes out to you
Each and every day
Happy is my life now
I wouldn't have it any other way

HAPPINESS

Happiness is a choice

That you and I can choose

You don't have to be unhappy

Or continue to have the blues

My Father has let me decide

Which way I want to go

I choose life and happiness

Any other way, I say no

Follow Him

❧

My heart truly belongs
To my God
My race in this life
Is sometimes hard
My spirit is willing
But my flesh tries
To keep killing
All thoughts of me
Following my Lord

CONFINED

Confined to within the ideas of my mind
Push them out, express yourself
It might take time
But don't give up or ever quit
You'll never know what you can do
With the gifts and talents
God has given you

ON MY WAY

You can't see what I'm going
to be
All you can see is my struggles.
Man she follows GOD and JE-SUS,
but all she has is trouble.
You really don't know
where I have been or
where I am going to go.
But God knows my purpose and
Des-tiny and is working on me
so it can show.
So the things that you see
that has happened to me
are all there for a special reason.
Some are long term, some are
 short term, but all are there
Just for a season.
Disasters you know, are opportunities
to grow, disguised with a mask as bad.
Stay in God's hand
 (cause He has the plan).
He'll take you from
what looks bad to glad.

HOPE IN GOD

When I laid
down as another day
has passed before me.
I reminisce about all the things
that have happened during my
awakening.
How the devil used no specific person
in my path, but used anyone
to cause me agony.
How yet another friend close
to me told me about his
recent tragedy.
How several friends continue to go through
trials, tribulations and situations.
How I fight hard to nurture my special
friendships with close
communication.
How I continue to wait for my cup
not only to fill up but to runneth over.
No, not one of these things
will get better by you carrying
a four leaf clover.

My hope in God is what I thought about
as I began to close my eyes.
I thought about HIS love HIS grace
HIS mercy and the hope that tomorrow
I will rise.
I thought about all the things He's
done for me like giving me friends.
People that have come to my rescue
when trouble has caused my light to dim.
I thought about what God says when
He said forget the past and that
trouble doesn't, but righteous people
do last.
I thought about all the times that
God has forgiven me, He said all
you have to do is ask.
I thought about the Special gift
that God gave to you and me.
All the reasons to have hope in Him
because He hung from that tree.

THE GIFT

You may be married
With children too
A loving husband and much to do
You might have many friends around
It seems like no time to be down
Yet still you feel a dark despair
Like no one loves you, no one cares
You feel an emptiness within your heart
A spot that must be filled by God
I have a friend that can help you too
It's the Holy-Spirit – a gift to you
He'll fill your heart with love and peace
From this day on you'll feel complete

Thank You Holy Spirit

CHAPTER THREE

Our God is an awesome God. I frequently sit by the river and just observe and take in all the natural wonders He created. How the wind blows yet you can't see it. How the massive waters stay where they were placed as does the stars, the moon and the sun; even how time was created to move forward, never going backwards.

THE WORLD DIDN'T HAPPEN BY CHANCE

The intelligent specific design by God
is not a random creation through
time and chance.
The exact calculation of the distance
between the earth and the sun
has proven
to have been done by a being
far far advanced.
The sun and the moon know
exactly when to appear and when
to move to another part of the earth.
The clouds sit waiting for their
command letting them know when it's
time for them to disperse.
The flowers and the trees bloom with ease
as if they were created with a brain
of their own.
All you have to do is count three months
and the weather
automatically gets in line with time
without being told.
Dots of light live in the sky at night
never falling once commanded
stay there.
Neither being visible each having
their distinct jobs ones called wind

the others called air.
Huge bodies of water massive by design
filled with all types of aquatic life.
Some you may eat, some look real neat
no one knows all of the kinds.
Creatures big and small seem to know all
there is to know in order to grow and survive.
Humans created from dust and with a breath of air
suddenly became alive.
All this was done of course by someone
why can't you believe it was God?
If you still take the stance
it was made just by chance
when you meet Him, He'll give you
the no nod

TIME
❧

The one thing you can't get back

Once it's gone away

No matter how much money you have

Or if you even pray

Not even as the President

Or a great big superstar

Time is gone once it's passed

No matter who you are

THE SUN

꧁

The rain has fallen constantly
Not one day's passed without
The drought is gone
The tides are high
Dreariness begins to mount
My friend the sun has been secluded
For many days have passed
There's nothing left
That isn't wet
To include the tall, tall grass
Today there was a sighting
Of the bright and shiny planet
It was the sun; it was just great
Don't take the days for granted

Nature

As the sound of each wave
Distinct in its movement
Washes itself up ashore
Mountains of green
Trees swaying in the breeze
Looking like soldiers prepared for war
Birds whistling and chasing
As if calling one another and playing
A game of tag
Bubbles up to the surface
From the fish he's been searching
As if to say, try and catch me if you can
Clouds of gray and white swirl
Shields the sun as it peeks
As it moves to the other side of the world
Rain drops fall not for long
Feel a wind not that strong
Beauty in nature God created
Nothing wrong

CHAPTER FOUR

As God stirred my heart to write poems concerning friends and family, my job was to put on paper what flowed out of my heart. As you will read, a few were written of friends who went to heaven. One is a response to a letter from my brother; another was words I had written for my son prior to him accepting Jesus. There's a poem about the birth of my niece's son, Immanuel. There's one about a dear lady that became an inspiration to me. Two were written, one about prayers from my minister and one special plea of prayer for my minister. Not only is all this in this chapter, but the story of what happened to me and my true love who passed away March 27, 2004, of Leukemia.

ANOTHER SLEEPLESS NIGHT

Another sleepless night
after hearing the
words that are becoming
all too common
She passed away today
Father, I know we each have
a date we will not miss
there's just no other way
I know once born
we live life, then die
But back to back to back to back
can you tell me why?
I know that you are
God of all
and love me very dearly
But now its moved from
only one to an average of five
deaths yearly
Although the pain of living life
can feel like weighted chains
In any situation that
comes my way
You're still the God That Reigns
You, made me Lord
yes with emotions
so it's okay to cry

I just can't get so stuck in grief
that with them I also die
From the first, which was my mom
I've changed so very much
You've given me, a mission
in life
and sealed it with Your touch
so no more should I take a count
of who has passed away
The thing that I must continue to do
is talk to all today
about Your love and about Your grace and
Your Only Begotten SON
and if accepted in their hearts
real joy when that death
date comes
So joy stealing devil you're a Loser again
Another one is still alive,
She belonged to God
given a brand new bod
In Heaven will she reside.
We Love You Ms. Anderson

A Poem For Brenda

When Church service began
you'd always find one special spot
where she liked to sit
Never in the front but three rows from the back,
this seat had the perfect fit
An employee, who worked, for twenty-eight years
deserves more than just a card
and although she's worked for every
department in the store
Shoe department is where she departed
For twenty-eight years every day that she reported
she came with a smile on her face
in spite of the walk that she took from
the bus stop
with Jean by her side keeping pace
There wasn't a time you'd ever find
a day without her answering with a laugh
Ask her anything no matter what it was
she always ended it with "aha"
We know the store, has replaced her
with someone, a person to fill the part
But no doubt about it the memory of Brenda
will never depart our hearts

THE LETTER

Got a letter today from
My youngest brother
Requesting information from
Me about my mother
he also asked if I would
Look
For a publishing company
To publish his book
He wanted to know what's
Wrong with him
For the third time in his life
He's in the Penn
He's planning to seek psychiatric
Help
For the curse in his life
He says he's been dealt
He's Jehovah witness, Christian
or Muslim
Three years in a row he's
Been at least one of them
Excuses were many
Accountability was none
If he lived like that
No wonder he's done
I will write back and will

Explain
In words that are
Simple and very plain
He can look in all the wrong
Places
And looking at things of
The past
Is time wasted
There's only one place
He should look
it's in a more than
2000 year old book
The Word of God is what
I mean He'll break that bondage
He'll
Make him clean
He'll renew his mind and
Change his heart
Even in the Penn he'll have
A brand new start
But first things first
He must receive
Jesus in his heart
And be relieved
Of all that pain of
Falling short
No more in life he'll
Be in court.

Erick My Son

❧

You live far, far, away
But you better believe
I always pray
For your safety, your health
and your total well being
From the conversations we have
I am now seeing
It's working for you
As well as for me
He said he would do
Whatever we please
For the moment, that's fine
Through prayers from mothers.
Don't wait too long my son
Don't be like the others.

SHEKIVA'S LABOR

Seen a little kid today
That reminded me of my niece
The little girl
Was about 2 years old
And didn't have all her teeth
She was chewing gum, but she wanted some
Just to hold in her hand
This brought back memories
Of the 80's
When my niece wanted to be
With her aunt
I've seen her grow
With my son you know
They're thirteen days apart
He's big and strong
Living on his own
One day, a family
He will start
You see, they're grown
And I've always known
Shekiva wanted a husband
And a family
She's got the first
Working on the birth

I'm waiting on the call
That says I'm an aunt
Again

IMMANUEL CHRISTIAN ANDERSON
Born 2 February 2005
1933 hrs, 7lbs, 5 oz 20"

DON'T SWEAT THE SMALL STUFF

Got a problem, feeling so sad
wondering why it happened to you
Now tired and weary from constantly fighting
and wondering what else can you do
You're following GOD but you still got robbed
and lost everything that you owned
Just found out you have to move in a month
cause the owner wants to sell her home
Your job is now moving must decide
if you're willing
to move your family
from state to state
These all sound like legitimate
problems that can cause you sadness
but hold on
Just a minute, now wait
Go to the hospital and visit a few
of the patients that are lying there
It'll put into perspective the problems you have
that you once thought
really was unfair
The afflictions are many, some you can see
but some are set deep within
The problem for these people
aren't things that are replaceable,
but will they see the sun once again

So when sadness and pity
come knocking at your door
before you decide to open it up to let them in
Go visit Ms. Wilborn in 403-1 you'll see gratefulness
and what it really means to depend
on God the Father and God the Son and God
The Holy Spirit
By the time you leave her room
your heart will be changed
Through her humor you'll finally get it.
Thanks Ms. Wilborn

PRAYED THROUGH

All the years I went to
This church
I have received many a
Prayer
Consistent attendance
wasn't one of my
Traits
My problems were evident
most years
Though things were so
wrong
The prayer was very
Strong
I just didn't seem to
Care
But one thing too many
Came at me from the
Enemy
So now I am always
There
Thanks to the staff
That has prayed
Me back glad
And now I am one of
 God's seekers
I love Him so much

I so need His touch
I also want to thank Minister Banks-Booker
She prayed me through
Break throughs
And shows me the way
To be an obedient servant
In an instant when called
She comes to help
Us all
May God bless her because
She deserves it.

Thanks for praying me through.

A Plea For Her

A person goes up to receive salvation
She's right there by their side
Another comes forward because they're having
Complications
She pleads to God to make things right
Any song being sung in the service by anyone
You can bet that she already knew it
Any time the Chaplain says - do this or go pray
she doesn't complain she just does it
supportive is she to all those that give
To the ministry with sermon or song
With encouraging words from the pew that really says
I agree and I like what's going on
This lady you see is so godly to me
Yet real with a sense of humor
She's special to me, those three things that I see
Not only in her, but my mother
That's why it's so easy to love her.
But then comes a time she's not at her prime
Because trouble has come inching forward
The devil's working hard to stop her real joy
Cause to stop her he has to destroy it
But now I come in with a plea to my friend
My Father my God and my Savior
You said "until now you haven't asked in My name"
So in JESUS name please do this favor

Please bless her family with all that she wants
But especially with all that she needs
She's helped many people in time of their Trouble
By this she has sown many seeds
So help her Father with Your heavenly touch
and give her a banquet of healing harvests
I thank you my Father for all of Your blessings
And these words You've given me
Your writing artist

MY SACRIFICE

There was a time in my life
when I did what I wanted
Not thinking or caring that I
soon would be haunted
By the turn my life took
that one fateful night
When my mom went to heaven
then things were not right
I went straight to rock bottom
no stops in between
Life couldn't go on
at least that's how it seemed.
I struggled with things
that seemed easy before
I stayed in the house
never walked out the door
The people I loved
meant nothing to me
Including my ex who was
special as can be.
I was dead but still walking
no one could I help
I was no good for anyone
I couldn't even help myself.
My doctor I saw for severe
headache pains

I was rushed to the hospital
being told I would die this day.

You see, I was severely depressed
And my heart showed the pain
I was going to die
But that's when He came.
He is my Father, my God and
My Friend
that's when my relationship with him
Really began
Out with the old, all things became
New
I had to start over, excluding my ex too
Then God gave me love, kindness
And care He showed me how to follow him
No matter whose there
It took a few years, but I'm no
Longer weak
God's given me the job to help
with the bleak
To show them the way just how

He showed me

Then one day we'll all be in heaven
With thee
I was full of joy, my contract
in sight

My book was coming along

With all the poems that I write.

Thank you God for blessing me
So
Just then I got hit, with another
Blow
My ex became ill his fate was
Unknown
Especially when bad blood cells called
Leukemia had grown
As soon as I heard, to his
Bedside I went
The devil tried to kill him, his energy
Was spent
He needed help quick, from Father
Above
I led him to the Lord and
Told of his love
He asked me to call and pray
For him each night
I knew in my heart he would be alright.
As time continued passing, improvement began
He's now cancer free
By the stroke of God's hand
My job's just beginning though
This poem's about to end
I must teach him and show him
How to live without sin
Our lives come full circle
From beginning to now
My God's in the center

We're no longer down.
What He's done for us He'll do it for you
As long as you stay
In continuous pursuit

That last phrase was written
In the middle of the month
I now need a new ending

Because of the turn that he took
Although the test that he took showed
His blood to be cancer free
For some unknown reason
His doc didn't agree
One too many treatments
Took his life from this earth
My Alex was gone, then I really
Began to hurt
My true love indeed, although he's
Been freed
I'm back in a familiar area
That causes me to grieve
In spite of the pain, his family
And I feel
We must try to remember
He no longer has to deal
With the troubles of life
And the illnesses that come
My Alex is in heaven
With my God having fun
I love you baby.

CHAPTER FIVE

Friendships, I believe, are gifts from God. They are necessary to help fulfill your life. I know my life's been richer because of them. God has placed people in my life as helpers, helpees and sometimes they even appear to become the test. Some are only for a season. Nonetheless, all are valuable in contributing to my life's journey, hence these poems.

September 20, 1999
EVERYONE BORN
❧

Everyone born lives a life

It may be long or short

We have a mother, we have a father

And we all have Jesus Christ

But we are not guaranteed any friends

Not even one or two

I thank you all for being there

To help me through and through

Some called, some came, some brought me food

And even a movie or two

Whatever I needed you were there

To help me make it through

This tiny little setback that had me down and out

But now I'm doing well again

And now its time to shout

I thank you God for all these friends, not one or two or three

But for many friends you sent my way, to be there just for me!!!

THANK YOU,
LOVE

Genuine Friendships

Are gifts from heaven above
Don't take them for granted
Nurture them with love
When time has passed
And the newness is gone
Don't be the kind of friend
That tries to move on
Each one that is special
And unique in its way
Can make a big difference
In your life each day
Your life is made up
Of family and friends
Anyone without these
Can quite understand
That life can be hard
And desperately lonely
But guess what my friend
You are not the only
Person to live life without friends
I will now tell you how this process begins
You must be your real self
At all times you see
To know the real person
Is the beginning of we
You treat her like gold

Of which you have none
Special she'll feel
Enjoying great fun
When things get real rough
And she's feeling down
Brighten up her day
If it means being a clown
Go to great lengths
To give her assurance
Show her you'll be there
For the endurance
After you've done all the things above
There won't be any doubt of you or your love
Your friendship will be
Content when it's quiet
To have your own genuine
Friendship, just try it

My Friend

A few short years ago
I can truly say
I got to know an extra special person
He measured his life
By the love he felt
For his children and his mother
He gives and helps others
Without rewards
Or favors in return
That's why I want to lend my shoulder
A friendship he has earned
He works a lot, his life is hard,
It's full of care and worry
Any good fortune that comes my way
Or even winning the lottery
Just know you'll be a part of it all
No fuss, no muss, no doubt
The character that you are today
Make me want to shout
Thank You Lord
For everything you've given us this life
And let you know I'm here for you
To ease the pain and strife
Of everyday life,
The cares and worries
That some times weigh you down

No matter what kind of downs you have
I'll always be around

GREATEST CHRISTIAN FRIEND

I wanted someone as my friend
Sent from God above
In spite of not hearing a word from Him
And not even feeling the love
I created a situation
That was totally wrong for me
And then I blamed my God
For what I truly did not see
I only knew that I needed someone
A friendship of my own
Although the person was right in place
I still felt all alone
I knew right then that I was wrong
And needed to say I'm sorry
I repented to God and asked Him please
Just show your love and glory
He sent someone into my path
That's been there all the time
I needed to learn a lesson or two
Before her light would shine
The bond began to take great form
And issues were laid to rest
I've found my friend
She's strong like me
And helps me through the mess
God said to me Sheryl my dear

I now have answered your prayer
Your friend and Christian sister is
None other than Ms. Taylor

CHAPTER SIX

Although not always pleasant, God has given me poems for several events that have taken place.

African American History Month

❧

African American History
Month is upon us once again
It started many years ago
With oppression and when
The only slave was a black man
The man who started this
Special month which actually
Started as a week
Is Dr. Carter G. Woodson
Titled the Father of Black History
The month represents many
Black people who dared
to take a stand
One such person was Harriet
Tubman that freed many
Slaves with her plan
another was Oseola McCarty
Who washed and ironed for
Seventy five years
She earned little income
But you know what she's done
She established a $150,000
Trust fund
For students to attend
The university then where she lived
in Hattiesburg, Mississippi

And what about Sarah Breedlove
Known as Madam C. J. Walker
The first African American
Woman, millionaire, anyone's ever heard of
Now we get to Thurgood Marshall
the first black Supreme Court
Justice
He overturned many separate
but equal laws
And won the case against
School segregation for us
And of course you all know
The man that was called
Martin Luther King, Jr.
He accepted the call
to fight for us all
For the Equality
God said was due us
There are many more people
That deserves to be mentioned
Because they were vital
To our history
Poets, and Writers and Bishops and Singers
And some even had inventions
There's one thing I found
That was common
Ground
They all leaned on The Holy Spirit
Now, many don't know what I'm
Talking about and some of
You just don't care

The only thing that this day
means to you
is what kind of food's over there
but if you were to go
To a place, they said no, your
Color's not allowed in here
You'd appreciate the
Blacks that have fought
in the past and you'd
Celebrate this month with
Sincere

GROUND ZERO-CROSS OF FREEDOM

Empty spaces which once held
the tallest buildings
in New York
tracks from which a subway
train once stopped
so no one would have to walk
buildings condemned and
unusable still two years
later
fenced in construction sites
working hard to make the
city better
passing through this location
will make you stop and think
about the pain and suffering
that brought some to the brink
of being captives of their own
fears and a loss
of being free
but no matter what they did to us
we would not let it be
the end of our freedom or to
have the choice to feel
especially once they found
that cross
in the rubble- made of steel

Thank you Military

The struggles of war
Things you've never been exposed to
Or even seen before
Kids without limbs
Or eyes for their vision
That's when the question of
Who made this decision?
Comes to mind as you fight on the line
To free a suppressed people
Who don't care if you die
A war so unconventional
You can't see the enemy
Is it him, is it her, no it's a pregnant lady
The fear of slaughter
From weapons of mass destruction
Gives you the drive
to locate the production
Of anything deadly that causes great harm
You've seen how it works
He's used them before
Your comrades are dying
To the left, to the right
Worse, some are captured
Don't know of their plight
Each day seems to become longer
Than the day before

After seeing the plight of these people
I understand why we're at war
God bless all you soldiers
Marines, sailors, and Navy
You've sacrificed a great deal
So we all can be free

Thank You

THE CHRISTMAS TREE

Years ago, my son and I
Were trying to enjoy the season
The air was brisk; the stores were bright
But that wasn't the only reason
You see my friend; it was Christmas time
And joy was all around us
The more we looked, the less we found
To fit our tiny budget
We wanted a tree that was big and tall
And full of many branches
Each day we looked, we could not find
A tree to suit our fancy
Instead of crying and feeling down
Because the Day was near
We said to God,
You know our desires
So won't You take us there
Early that morning we got in the car
And headed to a store
We didn't know where we were going
We haven't been before
 I pulled into this parking lot
 Shrugging my shoulders high
My son looked at me curiously,
And began to wonder why
The store that we were looking at

Sold wood planks, washers, and dryers
But then we looked around some more
And saw our hearts desire
We left that store with big, big, joy
Thanks to God above
My son and I, we thank you God
We found a tree we love

GRADUATION DAY

Graduation day
Is here my son,
You've made it to the top
I know it's not been easy for you
But I'm glad you didn't stop
Until you got to where you are
And I'm very proud to say
Nothing makes me happier
Than this - Your Special Day

CHAPTER SEVEN

The first poem can and will fit many, but this is the story of someone close to me. After accepting Jesus in their life, not only are they doing well, they have become non – detectable. What an awesome God we serve. Thank You JESUS. Otherwise, I consider this my miscellaneous chapter.

Can't Live Without It

Moving from place to place
Eating whatever's around
Sometimes not even sleeping at all
Or finding myself on the ground
I met many people but none of them friends
They gave me all I wanted
Come back tomorrow, we'll give you some more
You don't have to come out of your pocket
This treatment went on days at a time
and soon turned into months
But after this period of time had elapsed
I realized I was stuck on the junk
No more freebies, they have told me
Now I must work for my stuff
I started stealing, prostituting, and dealing
To pay for this habit that stuck
My health got real bad
I knew that I had
Acquired the HIV virus
My life was so bad I was constantly sad
My friends said you need God; now try it I did right away
And all I can say
I don't want to live without it
God in my life has made all things right
I want each of you to try it
If a friends what you need

He's all that indeed
You won't even have to buy it

DAD COME HOME

❧

So many dads' are not around
To see their children grow
The critical years of their life
The time when they will know
What kind of person they should become
Or things they shouldn't do
But how can one parent show it all
When really there should be two
So come home dads
You might be glad
To see the things you've missed
I'm sure your kid will greet you there
And give you a great big kiss

INTERACTIVE POETRY

No matter what I did
It wouldn't go away
It never was invited
I wish it wouldn't stay
At times it seems to be leaving
And others not at all
Can you guess what I'm talking about?
You think you know the call?

The key is to get rid of it
Before it brings you down
And once you do
Make sure you don't
Let it come back around
It's excess weight I'm referring to
In case you didn't know
I hope to be saying goodbye to mine
That's not how I want to grow

EXPECTATIONS

The expectations of all around you
Can pull you in too many directions
Trying to please even two or three
Can cause you to lose affection
The stress can be tough
Especially if too much
And may show a lot in your complexion
Be true to yourself
Before anyone else
You'll continue to have a connection

COLORFUL ATMOSPHERE

The colorful atmosphere of the environment
Lent itself to the cheerful disposition
Of all around me
Noisy chatter, music playing
So many choices, which abound me
Flags displayed on the windowpanes
Small, yet each of us knowing
It has big meaning
The allowance of time
To take all we need
All signs showing we still are free

My Aunt, My Mom

My aunt is gone, my mom is too
You wonder what their kids would do
Let's hope that they will come to be
Someone to be proud of
You see
They've left this earth, but not our lives
They want us to do most things right
Because they hope and pray that we
Will be in heaven - agree?
The choice is yours
The choice is mine
Where will your address be?

DEPRESSION SUFFERERS

I have a couple of friends
that have suffered from depression
they've gone through bouts
of loneliness
in spite of the love
being expressed to them
they cry at night or in the day
it doesn't matter who's around
the only thing that they know then
is the feeling of being down
they're sometimes labeled
cry babies
but really, it's considered a disease
so please, don't just ignore the signs
of them asking
somebody, help me please
they may go for days, or months or years
without evidence that it's there
then just one little episode
can throw them back into despair
their thought patterns change
their life's rearranged
looking for someone to blame
now it's a must, time to adjust

for all the friends and family in pain
but now I have a message
to tell you my friends
something I want all to know
Jesus was beat
holding his cross in the street
to keep all from sinking so low
He paid the price
with His life
Getting depressed is not right
It's a place
we don't have the right to go

May God give you strength
M.M. and E.P.

TATE PUBLISHING *& Enterprises*

Tate Publishing is commited to excellence in the publishing industry. Our staff of highly trained professionals, including editors, graphic designers, and marketing personnel, work together to produce the very finest books available. The company reflects the philosophy established by the founders, based on Psalms 68:11,

"THE LORD GAVE THE WORD AND GREAT WAS THE COMPANY OF THOSE WHO PUBLISHED IT."

If you would like further information, please call
1.888.361.9473
or visit our website
www.tatepublishing.com

TATE PUBLISHING *& Enterprises*, LLC
127 E. Trade Center Terrace
Mustang, Oklahoma 73064 USA